FINANCIAL INTELLIGENCE

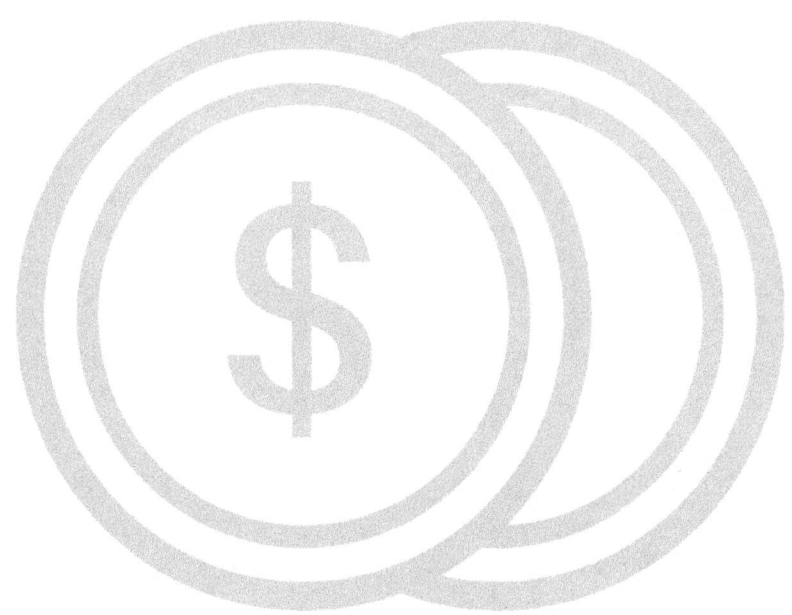

HOW TO MAKE MONEY ONLINE

INDEX

Introduction

Debunking the myths

Starting with

Types of legitimate online businesses

Service-based businesses

Affiliate Marketing

Selling on E-Bay

Earn money from membership sites

Make money selling products

Earn money by selling informational products

Making money by blogging

Earn money with desktop publishing

Creating a business from unusual ideas

Marketing your business online

Strategies to make your business successful

Website

Mailing of advertisements

Articles and other written content

Socializing for marketing

Miscellaneous marketing techniques

Marketing on the fun side

Final thoughts

FINANCIAL INTELLIGENCE

BOOK 1

FINANCIAL INTELLIGENCE

You'll get the same

Naturally, most of us, if not all of us, want and long for something better. It is part of us if we want a bigger car, a better house; buy good things for the family. We're still waiting for more, but to get what you don't have, you have to do something you've never done before.

That simply means:

Doing the same thing over and over again expecting different results! **CRAZY!!!!!!!**

As an employee, you can't stay in the same

job forever and expect a miracle to happen and your boss to suddenly give you a raise. You will be lucky that there is no downsizing in your company. Switching to another company will only provide a short-term solution to a long-term problem.

Sure, you can take a second or even third job, but do you have enough hours and stamina in a day to keep it up?

The bottom line: Exchanging time for money is not a good long-term financial sense. You keep increasing the hours just to win the rat race. That never leads to extraordinary results.

Raising their wages only puts them at a higher tax level. Their wages increase, but so do their household and auto expenses. How are you going to invest in yourself when all the time you spend working for a company, working for the government paying taxes and working for the bank paying for your house and car?

What if you get sick and can't work tomorrow? Will the government take care of your family?

I very much doubt it.

Isn't it time you took finances a little more seriously?

What is money?

You see, there are a lot of ideas of what people think money is.

Some say it's a form of measurement.

Yes, but a measure of what? Wealth? In the old days, people measured wealth by the number of cows, sheep, and horses they had. But do people today measure wealth by their cows and horses? What about slaves? Was there a time when labor was considered a hot commodity? Are slaves worth anything today? Is your money sitting in the bank to protect it if a recession hits the country? No, wealth cannot be measured by the base dollar.

Some say it is a form of power.

Yes, money can give you power, but if you are trapped on a deserted island forever with a great treasure, will that money mean anything to you? If someone offered you water and a helicopter to fly out of there, you would exchange all your money in a fraction of a second, so money is not a precise measure of power - it depends to a great extent on how and wisely you use it!

Many believe that it is the root of all evil... and many others assume this belief without much questioning.

Now, now, now, now... money is NOT the root of all evil (otherwise, why do you think churches still accept monetary donations and charity?). The love of money is the root of evil. Remember, money is an excellent servant, but a terrible master. If you are trading your life for money, money has power over your time and your life.

And unless you have the right financial information, lack of money can engender a lot of evil thoughts and a negative mentality, as seen mainly in cheats, thieves, criminals, breakups, scroungers, stingy, and more, to name a few.

But what is money really?

Money is an idea, backed by trust.

While money has been developed naturally by merchants in the old days to replace the questionable barter system, money today is literally invented by the rich and rich.

Entrepreneurs are willing to get rid of their money to buy other people's time. The time of other people, i.e. employees and the self-employed, becomes the asset of their employer and employers this invaluable resource to continue creating more wealth for themselves.

And here's the thing: while you work for money, you're enslaved by it!

90% of today's population is being

involuntarily enslaved.

What we don't realize is that there is a part of our soul that cannot be bought at any price. Would you cut off your little finger if your boss offered you 24 months of your salary immediately? You and I know we're worth more than that. But when you hear of people selling their body parts for cash in some countries, we can make our eyes pop out of orbits.

On the other hand, we occasionally sell a part of ourselves for money like a donkey and a carrot.

Before the change...

Now don't get me wrong: I'm not working on a job (I worked on one before I became an **ENTREPRENEUR**).

But let's face it: our current needs grow more than ever in any period of history. Prices go up, wages don't. There are more **baby boomers** than ever and they have very little pension to show for their decades of hard work.

And you can't guess how many people hate the unhealthy, hectic lifestyle of getting up early, dealing with stress for most of the day, joining traffic jams, spending more money and time traveling, enjoying very little rest, and repeating the viscosity cycle.

You definitely don't paint a good financial and lifestyle picture, do you?

The first step to change is to be aware of the problem. Awareness before change (or ABC for short) is necessary if you are going to make some change in life to start taking control of your financial life and then get out of the rat race.

We need consciousness to know what state we're in so we know where we're going.

Time and money

There are 4 types of people in the world:

1. No time, no money.

Most employees fall into this category. You can't go shopping on a Tuesday afternoon or fire your boss whenever you want. Most employees can't even save money on their pension for 3 years!

2. No time, lots of money.

Self-employed, professional and small business owners are in this category.

They are a little better off than the employee because they earn more, but they have to work even harder than the employees to keep up with declining profit margins, competition and service to their customers.

3. I have time, I don't have money.

Many farmers, school dropouts or vagrants have a lot of time but no money. Perhaps ignorance is a blessing, but without a stable source of income, how long can you last in the future?

4. I have time and a lot of money.

It is the category in which large entrepreneurs, owners and investors find themselves. Imagine, not having to work for money, but having money to work for you by investing it and making a profit by using your money to make money. **GLOORIOUS!!!!!!!!!**

Now ask yourself?

1. Which of the four categories do you currently fall into?

2. What category do you want to be in tomorrow?

Ways to Reach Wealth

2 Models of wealth creation

Everyone wants to earn more money, but people in general and is divided into two categories:

- Those who bring results after they are promised wealth first or those who bring results first, are then rewarded by others later. (EMPLOYED AND SELF-EMPLOYED).

- Those, entrepreneurs, business owners and investors.

There is no good or bad in this kind of thinking, but keep in mind: once again, you are trading your precious time for money. Instead of investing your time in an ASSET that generates money, you spend your time working on something that is short-term, of limited wealth, and does not give you much income after you stop working.

Also consider that this type of short-term vision will only produce limited or temporary results at best. Have you ever seen a security guard asleep at work when the boss is away?

In addition, the part where our emotions get the better of us is when at least our lives must be governed by the pursuit of the dollar. It is clear that when an employee is offered a higher salary, more medical benefits and longer vacations, his heart starts pumping faster.

A higher salary does not mean fewer financial problems. On the contrary, when your income increases, your commitments, your tax level, and the time you spend in your business increase. The higher your salary, the weaker your position will be because if your boss is paying you 5-digit income and calls for an emergency meeting, you'd better hurry to the office even if you're halfway through making love to your wife!

I think the best definition of an employee/boss relationship can be summed up like this.

An employee will only do the minimum to prevent the boss from firing them and a boss will only pay the minimum to prevent the employee from leaving.

Now let's explore the other group…

There are many creative people, inventors, entrepreneurs and business leaders who fall into this category.

An entrepreneur is someone who always has good ideas.

The first obstacle we have to overcome if we want to succeed in the second group is to stop working for money. What does this mean? Isn't making money part of having a good financial IQ?

What I mean by 'stop working for money' is that it's not working for free. Rather, it means working to gain the skills necessary to be a successful entreprener (or inventor, investor).

If you don't have contacts to run a business, where would be the best place to look for contacts? Of course, the customers of your competition.

What about product knowledge? Then work with a company that will teach you all the ins and outs of the tricks of the trade.

Not familiar with a factory production line?

Work on one! Learn how to handle ropes or how to handle factory workers.

Afraid to talk to people? Get a sales job where you'll be forced to talk to a lot of people. It's also a great way to develop perseverance!

Don't you know that the best education you can get is in real life? Not in the conference room.

The bottom line is that not everyone has what it takes to succeed as an entrepreneur.

It's not that easy. Many lack the perseverance, creative mentality, financial capabilities or people needed to do the job and usually give up too soon before the results can be seen. The quickest way to make those skills successful is to learn them hands-on and even get paid in the process! Don't be absorbed by what they pay you.

Again, let me emphasize:

Would you trade time for money in the short term? (Money stops coming when you stop) or Trade time and money for a long-term asset that generates income? (Even long after you stopped)

God created us with a brain. All we have to do is look around us and observe the problems that need to be overcome because every problem is an opportunity in disguise.

Everything depends on you. You may or may not see results in the short term, but by using our brains and the resources that surround us, we can create real value that others are willing to pay for what we have to offer.

3 Ways to Make Money

Let me summarize the 3 ways to make money

1. Trading time for money - employee, self-employed worker

2. Manifestation and use of creative ideas - inventors, artists, programmers

3. If you are a professional, have you ever explored the possibility of writing an e-book about your field of expertise? If well written, it could provide a new source of income, rather than having you spends your time serving your clients.

What about a computer programmer? You can come up with your own revolutionary product instead of selling your ideas to the company you work for.

What about real estate, rather than selling homes, you can pool sources of financing to buy cheap homes, increase their value, and sell them at a higher price. It only takes a little time and research to find good ideas.

FINANCIAL INTELLIGENCE-HOW TO MAKE MONEY ONLINE

Is money a problem? Look for loans if you can take the risk. Gather money from many investors or look for a subsidy. The sky is the limit when it comes to making money.

Again, how do you want to get wealth? Answer: It's up to you.

Main rule for investing

What does investing mean for people?

What comes to mind when you mention the word investment?

Does it mean putting your money into insurance, mutual funds, the stock market, or even high-yield investments?

Other people only think about investing when they are about to die and have left nothing for their offspring.

Some even tremble when they hear the word,

often stating that they have no money to invest or that they feel it is too complicated an issue to discuss.

Many people even invest a lot in health supplements, personal trainers and beauticians to live longer, be healthier or even look younger. Imagine the advertising budget of today's beauty companies.

These are all legitimate concerns when it comes to investing, but I'm talking about the most important investment a person can make in their life.

Invest in Yourself

The most important and primordial rule is

"Invest in yourself" - if you don't, who else will?

Your parents will only invest in your education until you leave college. But that's just the basic needs provided and it doesn't teach you important lessons about financial education.

Would you depend on colleges to teach you how to make money? Most colleges only teach you skills so you can earn money by working for other people. What about business school? Honestly, if business professors are such business experts, why do they still teach there instead of making a fortune in business?

Would your boss teach you to succeed in

business so that one day you'll be in their position?

You and only you have to be proactive enough to take that responsibility. You see, when you invest in yourself, it means assuming the importance of educating yourself. Education is not in the academic or technical sense, although they are necessary skills to be developed in life. Our education does not stop at the university.

For most working adults, their education enters a delay stage after leaving school. They stop learning and therefore stop growing. They only grow sideways by eating too many pizzas or take-away food during their busy lunch breaks.

We know IQ is important, don't we? But why aren't the world's smartest people the richest in the world? There are many accountants and financial planners running to their cars every night trying to overcome traffic jams after work! **They are not rich!**

What about Emotional Intelligence or Emotional Coefficient? Do working hard, having a great attitude and a positive mentality solve our financial situation? These are important when running a business, but let me use them:

If you're driving from Boston to New York using the wrong road map, you won't get to our destination no matter how fast you drive your car (working hard!). You can work harder, but you'll only get to the wrong destination faster. You may have the best attitude in the world or the most positive mentality, but you still won't make it to New York (although the trip wouldn't bother you since you feel positive about it).

The importance of financial education You should invest FIRST in your financial IQ.

Having a good financial IQ is not about saving tons of money or depositing it in mutual funds. It's developing a healthy money relationship and building a wealth of assets that will generate money for you.

What is needed to develop your financial IQ?

Delayed gratification is one of the most important aspects for the development of your financial IQ. Let's take this as a hypothetical example.

Would you pay for a pint of milk or a cow?

If you buy milk, it is consumed and it is over. You will have to buy the milk over and over again when it is finished. Even if milk costs less than a cow, in the long run you will continue to buy milk over and over again.

Now, if a cow cost 50 times more than milk, you could pay for the nose when you buy the cow, but after consuming 50 pints of milk from the cow, you would reach the break-even point in your investment and save more money in the future. In fact, the cow could give birth to 2 or more calves and you could select one of them for profit!

Got the idea?

EVERYONE is capable of creating wealth. When you take an old car and give it a general overhaul, paint it with a new coat of paint, and change a few more parts to get it working again, you could select that car for more money than if it were just an old, ramshackle car. You would have created wealth in the process!

How about a farm? If you turned a farm into a holiday resort in the countryside, wouldn't it increase the value of farmland?

It's the same principle for cooks, computer programmers and craftsmen. The sum of the whole is greater than the parts. We are all capable of creating wealth even out of nothing and that is the first step to making our creative juices flow.

The value of anything is defined by supply and demand.

You don't need a bachelor's degree in economics to understand this. Money is just an idea.

Remember the example of the desert island? The real measure of money is not the cents or dollars it represents.

If you have developed a product that people want, would you pay them more than usual? Would you apply your skills to create good assets?

The bottom line is this:

Invest in assets that add long-term value. Anything that brings you more income is an advantage. Don't invest too much in liabilities like cars or boats.

(If you lost your job tomorrow and can't pay for your house, is your house an asset or a liability?) Are you willing to leave your comfort zone and pay the price of the financial IQ? Or ignore the signs of the times and expect your boss, government and bank to take financial care of you for the rest of your life, living below your means and never taking risks to improve your family's future?.

How to get out of a financial mess

There are two methods I can recommend to get out of a financial mess.

Defensive Strategies

The first is defensive:

Reduce what you are already spending. You can't start a business in a financial mess. Cash flow is more important than income. And you need to have a lot of cash flow out of your pockets if you want to succeed.

Here are some of the things you can reduce

- Smoking - if you can't quit, simply reduce your consumption of a few cigarettes.

- Alcohol - alcohol can drain your finances faster than a running faucet.

- Night out - spending a few nights at home thinking about making more money.

- Betting - if you plan to bet, it's better to bet on a business.

- Vacation and country clubs - you won't die without a few memberships.

- Food - eat healthy and you can think more clearly.

- Laziness - the biggest thing that will stop you!

The most important thing of all is that you don't buy anything that constitutes a risk. A liability is anything that takes money out of your pocket no matter what it's worth in the future. Think in terms of cash flow. What can I invest in today to raise funds tomorrow?

Now let's move on to offensive strategies:

Offensive Strategies

One of the best, low-cost ways to invest in your business skills is to join a network marketing company. There are many other options, such as starting a traditional business or even an online business.

But if you want to guarantee something concrete where business skills are a concern, my opinion is about Network Marketing.

Regardless of what you've heard about this industry or how much money people have lost there, the main reason I would recommend everyone to invest in a network marketing company is because of what you can learn there, and not because of the amount of money you can make (although it would be fantastic if you can make a living from it).

You see, network marketing companies are the only place where people share their trade secrets for **FREE**. It's logical because for your bottom line to succeed, they'll also want you to succeed! Therefore, they will not refrain from teaching you the skills of a businessman.

In addition, the relatively low cost of investing in a network marketing company will surprise you by what you can learn from the price you are paying (a few bottles of vitamins and a business kit for the experience of a lifetime!). They patiently train you in the business attitudes and skills you need to succeed in this industry.

Basically, you can't succeed in network marketing with an employee's mentality. A network marketing company will train you in sales, communication, teamwork, leadership, positive thinking, self-improvement, investment of time and money, as well as the support of your up line as a personal trainer and mentor. I dare say that even if you don't earn a penny, but have diligently participated in their program, the skills you develop will last a lifetime.

You can also develop skills by linking up with an insurance agency. The work can be very hard, but those companies will also teach you the same skills as the previous ones and may also give you some advice on financial planning.

How about an Internet business? If you are computer literate, Internet businesses offer a low-cost, high-margin business that can earn a lot of money and access a global market.

Other places where you can learn about business skills can be found in financial planning courses, real estate investment courses, time management courses and much more.

All this I have suggested will be the safest way to start a new business. You are only spending a few hundred to thousands of dollars on start-up and education.

A traditional business can be too risky for someone without commercial experience.

You invest tens of thousands of dollars and may have difficulty getting to the break-even point. But once you've developed the skills above, you'll have a greater chance of success.

Most important of all, in addition to a good learning attitude, are the people you relate to.

It's been said before; you're the sum of the five people you spend the most time with!

This is very hard to swallow, but imagine if you start talking to your five beer-drinking and poker friends that you want to go out on your own and make a fortune, what would they say? They'd laugh at their socks before shattering your ego into a thousand pieces!

In the heart of man lies jealousy. They don't want to see the people around them succeed. If you succeed, it makes them look bad. They know in their hearts that they're not going anywhere, but they embrace that lifestyle and drag you along with them. They will steal your dream, and they will steal your financial freedom if you are not careful!

The key point to remember is: They only mingle with positive-thinking people!

Positive thinking is not a desire. A desirous thinker is a dreamer who does not act. Positive thinking is backed by action and you will feel the energy of the people who believe in you and support your dreams.

If you walk with ducks, you will croak... but if you walk with eagles, you will rise!

So start looking for people who follow your vision or who want to grow with you.

Finally, you must **BELIEVE IN YOURSELF!**

The task of getting out of your comfort zone can seem frightening and many will not support your sleep. They may even go on the offensive even if you don't share your dream. That person may even be your parents or spouse. Then you'll face the question, is my financial freedom worth the price I'm paying now? Can I live another day with the same routine, the same job, the same pay or the same job? If the answer is no, then take action NOW. Not tomorrow, you will wake up and forget your dream.

Write your wish on a piece of paper and hold on to it firmly every day. Share it with someone positive and take the first step.

You won't regret it.

For your financial freedom!!!

HOW TO MAKE MONEY ONLINE

BOOK 2

HOW TO MAKE MONEY ONLINE

Introduction

We live in an uncertain world, but there is one thing we know to be true... and that is that times are hard. Inflation is rising on almost every front. You're struggling to make ends meet, but just when you think you're making progress, life throws you a slap in the face.

Bills are piling up, the cost of necessities is rising and gas prices continue to fluctuate. You've known a time in your life when working for a living seems to push you further into a hole you can't dig.

Take a deep breath... Relax... and read this

book, as it will help you realize that there is an answer to this maddening situation you have found yourself in. You can make a living without burying yourself in an avalanche. You can get up and see the soul-warming sunlight that others have seen.

Take comfort in knowing that inner peace is within your reach; and we will show you how to find it by getting your income online.

Debunking the myths

Since we are talking about making a living online; it is important that the problems of Internet fraud are addressed. You want to be aware, but there is no reason to let doubts stand in your way when deciding which online business path to take.

Scams, spam and fraud seem to be synonymous with the word internet these days. Many cynics put up this way of making a living just because the Internet is involved. They will shout scam or fraud on the rooftops when they hear about any kind of opportunity to make money online.

While there are scams in online commercial cyberspace, there are many legitimate opportunities to explore. Research will provide you with a wealth of information and tips for detecting these scams, so you can move forward and make a living from the comfort of your home.

Over the years, scams and fraud have grown in all areas of the Internet, which has understandably made people concerned about doing anything online. There are legitimate ways to make money on the Internet - many people have done so successfully and continue to do so today. So don't let this opportunity pass you by because of lingering doubts.

This book will show you how you can earn money legitimately and avoid those nasty scams that could take advantage of you.

The more informed you are about Internet scams, the safer you will be when looking for an online business. Take the lead and control the future of your business before someone tries to take advantage of you. Let's explode some of the myths of the scam!

Here are some of the popular statements made by most Internet scams and the truth behind them:

Myth: "Make money overnight!" These scams promise you a way to make money while you sleep. They make it seem like there's little work involved in getting this.

Truth: While it is possible to do this, it will take a lot of work and a lot of dedication to make this claim. Most online businesses will take a while to get started, but in the end it will be worth your effort.

Myth: "Turn your computer into an ATM machine to make money!" - Actually, there are many statements that begin with this kind of sales pitch.

True: the statement itself may be true, but beware of a sales pitch that starts this way. Most online business opportunities sell the business itself. Scammers tend to sell the benefit of making money. Usually, in that case, there really is no business for you. For the con artist, they are making money from people who pay them for what they say they will give them.

Myth: "Start your business for free. There's no money involved!" They promote the fact that you can start a business with absolutely no money in start-up fees.

Truth: This type of scam will scream the "no money involved" statement, but then turn around and ask you to pay them a certain amount of information about how to start a business for free. Hmm... Aren't they contradicting themselves? There will be some costs to start a business, but they rarely break the bank.

Myth: "Start writing at home for a living": this statement is similar to many others on the Internet that claim you can start a business from home with your typing or, in some cases, your data entry skills.

Truth: Yes, you can make money by writing or entering data from home. It's best to offer these services to your customers and avoid paying scammers for information on how to do it. You can find out how to do this, with your own free research!

There are many more scam opportunities, but these will give you some ideas about how these scams work and who likes to take advantage. Know your options and don't be afraid to investigate any opportunities you are not comfortable with.

Starting with

Fear of the start-up process tends to make people delay starting a business of their own. That fear usually boils down to the fact that they simply don't know how to do it or where to start. This report will help you with this process so that you can calm your fears and get through the startup phase easily.

Let's start with some frequently asked questions that most newbie's have in the start-up process.

"Do I have to have special skills or qualifications to start my own business?

You will need to have some knowledge in the field you are embarking on, but you do not need to have any college or business degree to get started in your own business. Of course, it will depend on the type of business you want to start.

A simple investigation into the field in which your potential business will be located will be enough to give you what you need in most cases. If you plan to offer a service such as web design, etc. you should have some skills in that area before trying to start your business.

College degrees and experience are always

helpful in getting experience in a field, but generally you don't need a degree to have your own online business. Knowledge has more power online, so it will be more important to read everything you can get your hands on that deals with your field.

Will it cost a lot of money?

Starting your own online business generally does not cost a lot of money. The money you invest is mainly for a computer, internet access and a website. Any other costs will be based on the type of business you want to get into.

The businesses you will sell items you have created will take some money to store the inventory items, but great deals can be found on the Internet for this purpose. If you plan to sell a service, such as web design, you will need to add software programs to your list of tools to buy.

For the most part, you won't have to go to your local bank and beg them to offer you a loan. Find the best deals on the items you need for the business you choose and you won't have to worry about the interest rates a loan would add to your budget.

"Will I still be able to start my own online business, even if I never operated my own business before?

Absolutely. Hundreds of Internet sellers have started their own businesses and have been successful without any previous business experience. Again, it all adds up to the amount of time and effort you put into your research.

The Internet itself has a great deal of information at your fingertips to help you learn all aspects of the business you want to start. You can find tips, tricks and all kinds of information from people who have been there and done that, so use this resource to get the power that will give you the knowledge.

"How much money can I make from an online business?

This will vary on many factors. What business you start, how much time and effort you put into it, and the return on investment in what you are offering; all play a role in what you will essentially do.

Some Internet sellers earn a six-figure income, while others earn the same amount that a full-time fast food worker usually does. No matter how much your business generates, you'll still be ahead of those who travel to your jobs. The money they spend on gasoline, work clothes and meals, etc. is money that goes into their pocket and not someone else's.

"Do I really need a website?"

You will need a website to run your business. You will need to sell your products or show potential customers what services you have to offer. It serves as your "office" or "store" would, only you won't need to rent expensive space in a building to use it for your online business.

Websites are fairly easy to create if you use one of the many website design software programs or website creation services. If you wish, you can also hire a web designer to create an excellent site for your business, so don't let your lack of web design skills stop you.

"Do I need special business licenses to run an online business?

You will need to check with your local government agencies to determine what you will need in your area. Each area is different, so it is best to check and see what you need before you start your business.

"I'm nervous about taking money from customers. What if I screw up the payment processing system?

If you are selling items, you will want to use an online payment system such as PayPal or Clickbank. These programs will take the entire payment process for you, including refunds. The shopping cart software will often come with a web build program, so take advantage of that option.

Types of legitimate online businesses

There are several types of online businesses you can choose from to get started. You should check each option and see which one suits your needs before continuing. Here are some of the most popular online businesses that people get involved in and what each one entails:

Service-based businesses

A service-based business is one that offers some form of service to potential customers.

Some of these include:

- Writing
- Web Design
- Accounting / Bookkeeping
- Virtual Assistant

Other small business owners find it difficult to carry out all their business tasks themselves, so they subcontract these projects to someone else. They look for people to provide the services they need for them.

If you have experience in some of these areas, you can offer it as a service by starting your own business by selling yourself. For example, if you have some experience in writing and can write well, you can offer that as a service to other people who need to write on their sites.

What skills are needed?

Depending on the type of service you choose to provide to your potential customers, you should have some skill at your disposal. You don't need to have educational degrees to perform these services, but customers like to see that you have some kind of experience to complete the tasks they need to do.

Working online does not provide the face-to-face contact that physical companies have when hiring employees. Trust becomes a little more difficult online, so people like to know that the person they are hiring has skills and knowledge in a particular field.

While it is not necessary to have more than 10 years of experience in providing a service, the fact that you have done it before and have some testimonials to support that claim helps enormously.

What tools are needed?

The tools you need will depend on the type of services you plan to provide. The most common ones that most service-based businesses should have are

- Computer
- Reliable Internet access
- Phone
- Email program

- Website

There will probably also be some software programs to obtain. Each service uses a few different ones, but most need a word processing program, an Excel program, and some use a web design program.

You should consider an instant messaging program for those customers who like to be able to contact you instantly without having to use the phone to call or wait for an email response.

How do you get started?

The first thing you need to do is decide what type of service you plan to offer your customers. Write down anything you can think of that shows you have some experience or knowledge in that particular field.

Then, create your website. Showcase your skills or experience on your site and give customers testimonials from others who have used your skills and are satisfied with the results. Post your rates and any other information about how you run your business.

Market your site in various places on the Internet so that your online business is available for potential customers to find and consult. When customers contact you to sign up for any service they need, reiterate how things are going. For example, let them know how they will be billed for the work done and how much it will cost, etc.

It will take a while to build up a list of regular customers, so don't expect to make tons of money right away. Give it time and keep promoting your service-based business until you get to the point where you practically reject customers because you are too busy.

Running a service-based business is a perfect option for those who already perform that service in another job. In most cases, you could make more money offering those services online than you can by working in a physical position.

Affiliate Marketing

This is an online business where you use your sales and marketing expertise to get consumers to buy other people's products and earn income from the sale you made. Usually, you would earn a predetermined amount of money based on the sales you make of those products, but in some cases, you may be able to make money from the clicks on your site that lead consumers to the affiliate websites.

Sometimes you can make money by having customers sign up to receive items on the affiliate sites, such as newsletters, etc. Each affiliate program will discuss this in more detail about how they work, so when you sign up for their program, be sure to check out how your process works. This will be done through an affiliate link that you will be provided to place on your site.

What skills are useful?

You don't have to be a salesman or saleswoman to be an affiliate salesman. However, knowledge about how to do these things will be important. Learn all you can about how online marketing works and learn how to be a successful affiliate marketer from other top marketers.

It will take a lot of hard work and dedication to make your affiliate marketing business successful. If you don't have the time or desire to work hard, don't consider this to be your online business.

What tools do you need?

The tools needed will be minimal. In addition to the usual computer with reliable Internet access, you will need a website to sell the affiliate products. You will not have to stock up on the products, just to sell them.

Your website will need new content on a regular basis, so be prepared to write some articles yourself or hire someone to do it for you. A blog to link to your site will also be useful for the search engines to be happy with you.

How do you get started?

You'll need to determine what niche you have for your affiliate marketing website. This helps you stand out from your competitors. For example, you could use nutrition as your niche. Then create a website based on the niche you chose for your business.

Then find affiliate products to sell from that site. Make sure the products you decide to sell for your business are related in some way to the niche you have chosen for your affiliate marketing business.

Then, if your niche is in the nutritional field, you will want to offer affiliate products that are related in some way to nutrition. If you do not offer related products in your business, you run the risk of appearing unprofessional and the search engines will not be very happy with you either.

There are many people who make good money from this type of business. It is important to remember that most of the work you will have in this type of business will be marketing your website for consumers to find. When they find you, your site should be able to get them interested in your products to the point where they will buy using your links.

Selling on E-Bay

This is another popular online business that

many people start with. E-Bay is a popular online auction website that millions of people use every day to find good deals on the items they are looking for.

You can sell anything you have at home, as well as sell items using a direct shipping method. If you do a search on the e-bay site, you will see a wide variety of items that people are selling. These could be used items or new items that come from wholesalers. Either way, people will pay good money if you provide them with what they are looking for.

Some people go so far as to buy items at flea markets and garage sales for the sole purpose of reselling them on e-bay for a profit.

What skills are useful?

There aren't many skills you'd need to sell items on e-bay. The ability to market your items will be the most important. People can do a search on the site for the items you are selling, but if you want to make money in this type of business, you will want to market those items elsewhere for people to find.

If you sell items from your home, you should be able to take a good picture of the item so people can see what shape it is in.

What tools do you need?

Really, the only tools you need to start this type of business is an e-bay account to sell your items. If you plan to use a direct shipping method, you will need to find a wholesaler who will ship the items directly to the customers.

You will need access to a computer with reliable Internet access to track your sales. You will also need an online account such as PayPal to receive money from your customers.

How do you get started?

Sign up for an E-Bay account that allows you to sell through them. Plan to buy items from the site as well to help you build your user qualifications, so people will have a little more confidence in buying from you.

Post photos, if possible, of the items you want to sell. Items that have a photo of items sell much faster than those that don't. People like to see what they're buying, so offer them the best possible photo quality.

Check out all the informational materials, as well as the rules on the E-Bay website, for tips on how to make more sales and how the selling process works on the site.

Selling on E-Bay is a great way to start your own online business. This gives you your first contact with an online business without having to have a lot of equipment to start with. Plus, you get the benefit of getting rid of the items that clutter up your home while making a little money.

Earn money from membership sites

Some online business owners earn money by selling memberships to their websites. People buy memberships to access content that the website owner provides on a regular basis.

For example, you may offer memberships to Internet users who need items for your websites. The memberships would have to be renewed every few months or so depending on how good your memberships are. Each time someone renews your membership, you make more money.

The profit potential for this type of business is quite high. It won't cost you much to provide your members with informational items, but you can charge them a good amount to access them, which gives you a profit that keeps on giving.

What skills are useful?

Marketing skills will be the most useful. Getting those Internet users to access your site to buy your memberships is what will make you money. Having some knowledge about how to run a website could also be useful to make your site run smoothly for your members.

You may want to have some knowledge of the products you offer. For example, if you are offering items to your members, you should know what makes an item good and how they work for different purposes.

What tools are needed?

You will need a high quality website to handle the demands that the membership site will bring. You must provide excellent service in case something goes wrong with the site. There are some membership site management software programs that can help you set up a membership site for less than $100.

Site content is another tool you will need. You should provide your paying members with new content to use regularly. This could be in the form of written articles, software programs or even online games, depending on what you plan to give your members.

How do you get started?

You will need to plan your membership site in advance. What do you plan to offer your members? Will it be content, software, etc.? When you've made your decision, come up with a new and different angle to provide to your consumers.

You could provide content in a specific niche, such as nutrition, or you could offer a certain type of written content, whatever it takes to provide Internet users with a new angle. This helps you stand out from the crowd of competitors.

Next, create your membership site with a shopping cart feature to handle membership payments. Membership management software programs should include everything you need to run your business. All you would need is the content to give to your members.

The most important step will be to market your membership site so that people will find it. Marketing techniques will be discussed later in this report.

Membership sites can provide you with a means to earn residual income. If people are satisfied with what you give them, they will have no problem giving you their money to keep renewing their access to your site's content.

Make money selling products

This type of business can be done in different ways. One way is to create and sell your own products. Artisans often enter this type of business to sell their own creations to the Internet public. Scrap bookers also choose this path for their business.

Another way to sell products is by using an online store that sells other products. There would be no inventory of items to store in your home, nor do you have to ship anything directly from your own location. The products are ordered through the "store" you have set up and the wholesaler who provides them will ship the items directly to the customers for you.

What skills are useful?

The skills you should have are the ability to work hard and good customer service skills. You will spend a lot of your time marketing your websites, so potential customers will find you. You will need to have a good website set up to provide customers with everything they need when deciding whether or not to buy your products.

Customers will have questions about your products and may have some issues that you need to address, so good customer service skills will be essential. Establishing a good relationship with your customers will start the customer cycle by returning to buy more from you. Providing top-notch customer service will help you achieve that.

What tools are needed?

If you have chosen to sell products that you create yourself; you will need to stock an inventory of items to create them. Check with some vendors to find good deals on items that are purchased in bulk to help you save some money.

Of course, you will need a website and your customers will need to find your products, see what they are and have a way to order what you are offering. Make sure the site has a shopping cart feature to make the buying process easier for your business.

How do you get started?

The first thing you will want to do is decide what you are going to sell. Are you creating your own products to offer or do you plan to sell other products by using direct loaders?

If you plan to sell items that you create yourself, then you will need to research vendors for the inventory you will need to make those products. Replenish some in advance, so that when consumers start ordering your product, you can ship them immediately and not make them wait another day or two while you invent them.

When the planning stage is complete, you'll need to create your website to sell them. Make sure the site is easy to navigate and not so distracting that your business goes offline in a few seconds.

Of course, the last step in getting started in this business will be marketing your products, which will be discussed later in this report. This step is the most important if you want your business to be a success, so don't skimp on it.

Selling products is a great way to make money online. If you already create products to give away to friends and family, there's no reason why you shouldn't take the product online and start selling it.

If you like the idea of selling products, but don't want to create one for yourself or if you just don't feel like being creative, then you can achieve this type of business by having someone else send you products. Starting this way online gives you the flexibility to spend the necessary time with your family, but still make a living.

Earn money by selling informational products

The Internet is a great place to sell your knowledge. There are many people who will pay almost anything to get information they desperately want. If you have the knowledge they want, you could make a substantial income.

Information products come in many forms. It could be one of the following:

- Electronic books
- Electronic courses
- Tutorials
- Guides
- Podcasts

These are popular information products that are highly sought after by Internet users. If you have something to say, this could be the business for you.

What skills are useful?

You must have knowledge of the subject matter you will be presenting to your consumers. You won't need a PhD or anything else to do this, but having a good amount of knowledge in the field would be helpful.

The ability to market your materials will also be helpful. The more people you contact with your products, the more people will want to buy from you.

What tools will be needed?

The tools you need will depend on what you plan to provide. E-books and guides could be written in word processing software and then converted to a PDF document, which is the most popular type of document people want.

Automated response programs will be needed to create successful e-learning courses. Podcasts would need audio recording and editing software. Tutorials can be done in two different ways. You can use a PowerPoint presentation to present your material or you can use video tutorial software. Video tutorials are excellent for showing users how to use a specific program step by step.

You will also need websites and blogs to promote your information products.

How to get started?

You will need to decide on a theme for your product. What do you know most about what you could provide to your potential customers? When you know what you want to provide, research that topic to see if you can find a new and unique angle to present it.

Since there are many e-books, tutorials, etc. on the Internet for sale, you will need to find something new to offer your customers. They won't be so willing to give up their money if they don't think you have something new to offer them.

Write or record your information product and then edit it to your satisfaction. Once you have it the way you want it, you can start selling it. Create a blog or website to sell it.

Make sure the content of the web copy of the site attracts the attention of Internet users so they can buy what you are offering.

Hire a copywriter if you can afford one to write the copy to promote those materials. They can write content in a way that makes your product so desirable that anyone will want to buy it.

Creating informational products won't cost you much, but you can sell them for a good profit. This is a great way to earn income online while maintaining a flexible schedule that allows you to spend more time with your family.

Making money by blogging

Blogs started years ago as a way for people to connect with others and share images, stories and experiences. It was seen as a great personal journaling tool that could be used to make a mark on the Internet through their encounters.

Blogs evolved to become excellent marketing tools, as well as a means of making money. There are a few different ways to earn income from blogs. Here are a few:

Adsense ads: popular search engines offer a way to make a little extra money with any blog or website. The idea is to place these ads on your site and when a visitor clicks on an ad on your site, you earn a predetermined amount of money. The more clicks you can get from visitors to your site, the more you can do. There are some rules, so if you choose to follow this route, make sure you learn what not to do before you sign up for their programs.

Product reviews: There are some websites you can register with that can help you connect with other companies that need people to review their products and get some exposure on their blogs. Usually the main requirement for this is to have a blog that has been around for a while and has a good amount of visitors. Those companies would pay you a specific amount to review your product on their blog.

Contextual links: Some business owners or websites will pay a blogger to post one of their links on their blog posts. Owners may contact the blog author or a company acting as an intermediary. These companies will find blogs related to their business sites, so the links provided on the blogs will be search engine friendly. This is a great way to gain some extra traffic for a site.

Sell products: blogs are another way to sell your own products. Those who have businesses that sell home decor items or food items use blogs a lot to help sell their products and make more money online.

What skills would be useful?

There is not much skill involved in this type of business, except the ability to market your blog. You will want to research blogs as much as possible to learn some of the tricks of the trade to make your blog popular.

What tools would be needed?

Your primary tool, in addition to a computer

FINANCIAL INTELLIGENCE-HOW TO MAKE MONEY ONLINE

with an Internet connection, would be a blog. There are many blog programs to choose from. Some are free to set up, while others require a monthly or annual fee to get started.

The paid versions of the blogging programs can help you connect with other blogs and increase your blog traffic. The free versions are extremely easy to set up and most are extremely popular with bloggers, so finding people to connect with would not be too difficult.

How do I get started?

Register with a blog program and start posting to it. Make sure you're blogging regularly, which would be about twice a

FINANCIAL INTELLIGENCE-HOW TO MAKE MONEY ONLINE

week. Blogs that are not updated regularly tend to get lost in cyberspace.

Market your blog as much as possible. Subscribe to blog directories, enter other people's blog rolls, and comment on other blog authors' posts to get some exposure to your blog. The more traffic you can drive to your blog, the greater your chances of making blogs a lucrative way to make money.

Most blogging programs will have a log for Ad Sense ads already included in their settings, so getting started will be easy. If you want to provide product reviews and contextual links, you'll want to be blogging for a while and get a good amount of traffic.

When your blog is ready, look for companies that will help you connect with companies that want to pay to have their products reviewed or have their links inserted into your blog posts. Once you're set up, you can start earning additional revenue with your blog.

Blogging is an easy way to earn some extra money if you plan to work hard to market it. Those who succeed in blogging for money use all possible routes to make their blog well known in Internet communities. Those who do not, tend to earn only a few cents per week.

Become one of the most successful bloggers and turn your blog into your business and not just a hobby to participate in from time to time. Your wallet will thank you.

Make money by training others

A coach is one who takes his knowledge in a particular trade and shares it with others who also want to succeed in that field. Coaches can be experts in anything from writing to marketing to the business itself.

If you have good knowledge or experience in a particular area, you can become a coach quite easily and earn money doing so. There are many coaches who help others in web design, graphic design and even in the field of coaching.

A coach would offer tips and techniques to newcomers in that field and answer questions throughout their learning process.

What skills are useful?

The most important skill you should have for this type of business is the ability to be a good listener. You must also have a lot of patience for your customers. Those who hire you to train them want you to listen to their bad experiences and help them out of the mess they are in, no matter how strange they may seem.

To build a good relationship and credibility in this business, you must know your field well. If you have never designed a website before, being a web design coach would not be a good idea, because your lack of experience will be detected immediately and your confidence will be lost.

What tools will be needed?

You must have the following in this type of business:

- Computer
- Email program
- Website
- Informative content for your site.
- Shopping cart function for your site to handle payments
- Dedicated phone for business purposes.

Most of your conversations with customers will probably be through your email programs, but some people may feel more comfortable talking to you on a more individual basis, so you should include a phone on your tool list.

How do you get started?

Plan your business. What service will you offer that you are knowledgeable about? Get some articles and other written content created to place on a website to help build credibility and expert status for your business.

Explain on your site how your service works and how much your fee will be. Show some testimonials from other people who have used your services before and were satisfied with the results. Make your site easy to navigate so others don't get lost trying to find information about your coaching business.

Market your coaching business so that clients come to you. Plan the goals the client wants to achieve by using it and discuss how those goals will be achieved. Listen to their problems and questions and provide insightful answers and support to keep them moving toward their goals.

Coaches are highly sought after online for those who have good knowledge or experience in a particular area. Use what you know about a topic and provide a training service to others to help them become experts like you in the same field.

Making Money in the Genealogy Business

This is a perfect business opportunity for those who love to research and love to learn about our ancestors. Genealogists make a living creating family trees for other people who don't have the time or patience to do it themselves.

Almost everyone likes to know where they came from and what their ancestors did that could have left a mark on the world. You can take advantage of their curiosity by doing research for them and providing them with their family heritage.

What skills would be useful?

Excellent research and organizational skills will be a high priority. These skills are what genealogy is all about. You will need to know where and how to research each family's heritage and be able to place all the information in a format that is easy for your clients to understand.

What tools would be needed?

You would need a computer with a reliable Internet connection. You should subscribe to some of the best genealogy websites available for your research. You should also invest in some guides or attend some classes to learn some tips and tricks for researching family trees.

You would need a website to manage your business. Customers will need to know how you do your job and how much you charge. Provide some samples if possible to show customers how thorough your work is.

How do you get started?

Gather all your supplies and find genealogy websites to subscribe to. Create a website to sell your service and then start marketing your business to attract customers to your site.

Use your Internet resources for research, as well as local libraries, courts, and historical societies. You may need to interview people to access certain information, so you may need to find a phone to use.

Create your family tree document that contains all the family heritage information or use software programs that provide it.

If you like to do research and are interested in historical documents, then you should consider this type of business. Meet the demands that people have to discover their family history and make money doing something you love to do.

Earn money with desktop publishing

If you are a creative person and can use a

computer well, consider an online business with desktop publishing. This is where you can create documents, flyers, brochures, calendars, and ads.

All of these types of documents are created using one or two programs on your computer, so you won't need expensive machinery to create them.

There are many people who look for these creative pages for all sorts of uses and don't know how to create one. If you have some knowledge in this area, you can use it to earn money by providing them with these creations.

What skills are useful?

The ability to move around a computer and use various types of software programs are some skills you should have. You don't have to be an artist to be in this business, because everything is done using the computer.

What tools are needed?

In addition to a computer, you must have the following equipment:

- Desktop publishing software
- Photo-editing software
- Laser or colour printer
- Scanner
- High quality printer paper

Make sure you know how to use all the functions of your equipment properly so that you can provide the best quality service to your customers.

How to get started?

You should get all the equipment you need to run your business. Choose a niche to focus your marketing efforts and then create a website to reflect that niche. Your website should provide potential customers with samples of your work to showcase your expertise in this field.

You can also brush up on your skills by reading any tutorials or guides in the field of desktop publishing.

Desktop publishing can be a very rewarding business for anyone who undertakes and loves to achieve creations to make someone jealous. If you are one of those people and want something that gives you flexibility, this is the business to sign up for.

Creating a business from unusual ideas

We have discussed the more conventional means of starting an online business. There are also some unconventional means that should be considered. By unconventional, we mean those ideas that came up and were laughed at by others. Those people who took those ideas to the top and made a great living. These are some of those ideas that people thought would never take off:

Selling old seminars: a kid made a living finding and selling old seminars that originally sold for thousands of dollars.

Domain names: someone came up with the idea that they could sell a domain name service for other people. It sounds crazy, but the business took off for them. It turns out that some people needed that service.

Selling used engagement jewelry: reportedly, this idea came from someone who broke off their engagement, got the ring back but discovered they couldn't return it for its full value. They started a place for other people in the same boat to sell their jewelry and get back what they paid for it or as close to it as possible.

Selling butterflies for a living: Yes, it's possible, or at least that's what one person found out when someone bet him that he couldn't sell them. Not only did he win that bet, but he made a great deal on that little idea.

There are many more ideas that people have submitted and made work as an online business, so check your memory banks and see if there is an idea hidden there that no one would believe could work. It could simply prove them wrong...

Marketing your business online

Strategies to make your business successful

Now that you've learned a few different online businesses to choose from, you'll want to learn some ways to market your business so that you can succeed like many other Internet marketers who have gone the distance you want to go.

Let's explore some of the most popular marketing strategies for your online business.

Website

Your online business website is the perfect place to start. If there is one thing that could make or break your business, it would be the website itself. Here are some things that are important to know about your website for marketing purposes:

Domain name: the domain name is the address to find your site on the Internet. You want to choose a domain name that closely matches your site or business name. This helps any Internet user to find your business easily if they are looking for a certain topic. An exact match would be the best option, but if it is not available, try to find one that is as close as possible.

Keywords: use the best keywords to place within the content of your site. Keywords are words that Internet search engines use when they go to search engines to find information on a specific topic. The search engine will index the keywords and place them on the results page for a user. The higher your site is on the results page, the more likely the user will choose your site to visit.

Niche marketing: a niche reduces your business to market to a certain group of people. Limit your marketing efforts to a smaller group to help you deliver what your consumers want. Larger groups have too many people who have many different needs. This makes it difficult to get your audience interested in what you have. Smaller groups will be the people most likely to want what you have, so marketing will be much easier.

Your website should reflect the niche you choose for your business. If you are targeting mothers with young children, your site should reflect that. It would have graphics that would connect with mothers with young children and the site content should be written with something they can relate to. This will also help with search engines.

Blog: provide a blog to go with your site. It should relate to the theme of your business site. Personal blogs should not be used here. If you are using a blogging program that is not connected to your site, try to design the blog template to match your business site as closely as possible, so that it looks like the blog matches the site.

Blogs are another way of using search engines to gain visitors. When a visitor finds your blog, he or she can see that you have more information to offer on that topic elsewhere on your website, so he or she can click the provided link.

Mailing of advertisements

Emails are essential to any marketing campaign. That's how you keep your business and products fresh in the minds of your potential customers. Getting a visitor to visit your site is one thing, but getting them to remember you through the millions of other websites is all in itself; especially when they are interested in buying.

Emails are sent at regular intervals to provide information to website visitors to help build credibility and put your company's name on the front page. This can be done in two different ways. To get email addresses to send your messages, you will need to provide an optional email feature on your site so that people can sign up to receive updates on what you are offering or to get more information.

Newsletters: These are used to provide short articles on topics related to your business. For example, if you sell vitamins and minerals, your newsletter may offer articles on alternative health practices, etc. to show how important your product is to them.

Newsletters can be sent to your email boxes with the introduction of an article and a link where they can go to your site to read the rest of the article. This allows users to become familiar with your site and makes it easier to remember when they decide they want to buy something you are offering.

E-courses: You can have a registration function on your site for visitors to use to learn the basics about a subject. If you sell vitamin products, you can use an e-course to help teach your readers how to choose the best ones for different types of health problems.

E-courses are usually sent out over a period of 5-7 days and are often offered free of charge. This keeps your company's name in mind by reminding you every day that the e-course comes into your inbox.

Updates: for those who have purchased something from you or people who have registered for this feature, you can provide them with updates on your products, discounts, gifts, etc. This way, if you don't entice a visitor to buy your In the first visit they can see something later that catches their eye and attracts them to buy.

Updates can also help drive more traffic to your site. Those who have already signed up for your lists will have friends, family, neighbors and co-workers whom they can refer to your business by simply forwarding the messages.

Articles and other written content

In addition to providing good website content, articles and other written content can be used in a variety of ways to market your business. Here are some of those ways:

Article directories: Article directories provide excellent marketing tactics for your business. By writing and submitting an article related to your company's site, you can accomplish two things...

1. Credibility on the topic you have written about

2. Drive more traffic to your site by providing a link to your company's website in the

author biography section found in the article directory sites.

These directory sites generally rank well with the search engine results page, so someone who stumbles upon one of your articles submitted within a directory can find their way to your website for more information on that topic.

Articles placed in another site's newsletter or blog: By being a guest writer on someone else's blog or newsletter, you can communicate with a group of people looking for information on a topic.

You should provide a link to your site within these articles and then reciprocate the favor by having the other website owner provide the same type of articles in their newsletters or blogs.

Articles on Digg or similar sites: Having one of your articles submitted on Digg or a similar type of site will give you more access to your site. Digg is a site that provides articles that other Internet users have found to be good informational articles. Those articles that receive a large amount of "Diggs" will be sent to the home page where many users will view and review them. The link to your site could be included for those who want more information on the subject.

Offer e-books or guides: you can provide your consumers with information on a topic and include a link to your site to keep them familiar with your business. These can be offered for free or for a small fee.

The word Free can be a powerful word for any user and capture their attention quite easily. It would provide basic information on a subject and they might be interested in buying an e-book that has more detailed information on the same subject.

Socializing for marketing

One of the most successful ways to find the traffic you are looking for is to socialize with other like-minded people. These are the most popular ways to socialize for your marketing needs:

Blog comments: find other blogs that have the same type of topic as your website. Post a response on some of your posts. The link on your website will be associated with your name and those looking for more information on that topic will check out your site or blog and see what they have to offer.

Join forum communities: Find message board communities that have topics related to your website. Your website's link could go on the signature line allowing others to find their way to the site to see what you have. Check the board's rules first to make sure this is allowed.

By posting regularly on these forums, you can build credibility as an expert on that topic and gain some trust with some potential consumers who may be thinking of buying from you. Also, other board members can refer people who know about your site, so be sure to return anything you receive with these communities.

Social networking sites: Social networking sites include popular sites such as MySpace and Facebook. These sites attract people who are looking for other people interested in the same things they are.

Internet marketers use them all the time to connect with people in their target audience. People who have the same interest as you can communicate and start building trust with you. They will be more receptive to buying from someone in your "group" or they may pass on your business information to others they know.

Miscellaneous marketing techniques

Here are some other techniques to use in your marketing campaigns:

Affiliate programs: start your affiliate programs for your products. Let other people earn some money by marketing your products for you. More traffic will come to your site through someone else's efforts.

Learn how to start your own successful affiliate program and create a web page on your site for others to sign up to be your affiliates. This is something you can announce in your newsletters and update messages.

Adwords: search engines offer this feature to business owners to buy advertising space on search result pages. Every time someone clicks on that ad, the search engine will be charged a certain amount of money.

Because you are paying for the clicks, you will want to provide the most desirable ad possible to increase your return on investment. Poor ads can cost you money, because not everyone who clicks on these ads will want to buy. Keep track of these ads and remove or update them when necessary to avoid losing too much money for your business.

Word of mouth campaign: this is the easiest marketing technique there is. A simple word-of-mouth campaign will get people to pass on your business information to others, etc.

This works very well for local customers and clients to hear about your business and pass it on to others who may be looking for the same products or information. This is also an inexpensive way to market your business.

Use press releases: this option can be used if you are just opening your doors or if you are offering a discount or a special sale. Press releases are sent to sites that post them for Internet users looking for specific information.

They are written as if they were news, and they display their "news" with eye-catching, attention-grabbing headlines and information. Your sale, discount or business start-up would have a lot of exposure to potential consumers and customers.

A well-written press release to announce what you are offering may be just what you need to attract a large amount of traffic to your company's website. Consider doing one periodically to help keep your company's name fresh in people's minds.

Place an ad in the local newspaper: There is no rule that says you only have to market on the Internet, so why not try to market locally by placing ads in local newspapers? Those ads are seen by most people who live within that area and receive that document.

Sometimes companies get their first sales transactions from local customers, so don't neglect your local area when planning your marketing campaign.

Podcasting: Podcasting is audio content that people use to provide information that people hear rather than read. It gives them a different medium to learn about a topic that interests them. People love the option of podcasting to listen while doing something else and not have to be glued to their computer screen.

Your business gains credibility and trust among listeners. Those listeners can become customers, so your website will be linked to the audio program.

Marketing on the fun side

People love to have fun, so why not provide them with your marketing techniques? Here are some ways you can give it to them:

Organize a contest: people will come from all over when a contest is announced. Run one on your blog or site to generate more traffic. You'll need to market the contest heavily so people will know, but once they know they'll come running.

Make your contest a fun one that almost anyone can participate in. Offer a prize that is worthwhile for the winner of the contest. If you don't, people won't come running the next time you hold a contest or something for your business.

A contest could be quizzes to take, an Internet safari to enter, or just a drawing to draw names.

Have promotional products with your company's logo: websites like Café express will make products like T-shirts, pens, mugs and even hats with your logo. Some of these can be given away or you can have Internet visitors buy them through a link on your site.

These promotional items can be displayed so that anyone who comes in contact with that item will see your logo and be curious about whose business it is. They can then search your site to find out exactly what you offer.

Final thoughts

Anyone can run their own online business, whether they have extensive business experience or not. All you really need is the drive to succeed and the ability to work hard and learn all you can about the business you decide to enter.

With the many options available to online businesses, you can find one that meets your needs and skills that you should bring to the table. Use every marketing method you can to get your business into every corner of the Internet world and drive traffic to your site.

The hard work and sweat you put into it

initially will pay off in the end, as you can start to relax a little and maybe hire someone else to do some of your daily tasks for you. What better way to make a living than to hire someone else to do your hard work for you?

The Internet offers more and more opportunities for business owners to make money every day, so why not get in the car now and start reaping some of the rewards that other Internet sellers are achieving? If they can do it with little business experience, you can do it too.